Contents

Acknowledgements

We are grateful to Lindsay MacHardy, Health Service Programme Manager at the Health Education Board for Scotland, and Lesley Moodie, Education and Training Manager, for their comments and suggestions throughout the production of this book. We would also like to thank Dr James Hartley, Professor of Psychology at the University of Keele, and our colleagues working in patient education who checked the accuracy of the text. Finally, our thanks to the people who helped with piloting the book for the constructive criticism they gave us through the researcher.

Introduction

This book aims to give you some general principles for producing more effective patient education leaflets. It is based on a literature review and on advice from health educators and researchers. We have tried to make the book relevant to everyone who is thinking of producing a leaflet, regardless of length or the budget available. For the sake of simplicity, we have used the term leaflet to cover all written materials for patients, from an A4 photocopied sheet to a glossy pamphlet.

We have not included advice about specialist topics such as producing leaflets in languages other than English for ethnic minority groups, although the general principles outlined here will still apply. Some books and articles which do give specialist advice are listed in the section on further reading at the end of the book.

Each chapter in the book describes a stage in the process of producing a leaflet. However, the amount of time you spend on each stage will depend on what you are trying to achieve with your leaflet.

As well as using the book as a guide, we recommend that you take part in training to get practical experience of producing a leaflet. A course called 'Getting your message across' has been developed by Fife Healthcare NHS Trust Health Promotion Department and the Health Education Board for Scotland. Your local health promotion department should be able to tell you about this. You will find their address and telephone number on page 59 and 60.

Before you begin

Introduction

Before you begin to write your leaflet there are 6 questions you need to consider:

• Is new information needed?

• Is a leaflet the best way of meeting that need?

• What will your leaflet aim to achieve?

• How will you find the information you need to include in your leaflet?

• How will you distribute the leaflet?

• How much will it cost to produce?

In this chapter we look at each of these questions in turn and suggest some ways of addressing them.

Is there a need for new information?

There are many reasons why you may want to provide information for your patients. For example, you might be aware that many of them ask the same questions about a particular condition or about the treatment for it. Or it may be that you are setting up a new service which your patients won't know is available unless you tell them about it.

But before you decide there is a need, you should check if suitable information is already available; it would be pointless to do it all again. Your local health promotion department or Patient Education Scotland can help you find out what is already available (addresses and contact numbers on pages 59 and 60). Ask your patients to look at any information you find. They will be able to tell you whether or not it is useful.

If you decide to produce your own information, it is still a good idea to get copies of anything that is already available. This will help you decide what you want to include.

Is a leaflet appropriate?

Leaflets have disadvantages as well as advantages, so this may not be the best way of providing your patients with information.

Some of the **advantages of leaflets** are:

• they reinforce verbal information and help people remember it;

• they can give more details than you can give verbally;

• they can be kept for future reference;

• patients can share the information with their family, carer or friends;

• a leaflet makes sure that each patient gets the same information.

Some of the **disadvantages of leaflets** are:

• they may be used instead of discussion with patients;

• they can't be tailored to the needs of each individual patient;

• they may not be the best way of giving complicated instructions;

• producing a leaflet costs time, effort and money;

• the information in a leaflet can go out of date quickly;

• people's ability to read varies.

You need to think about these advantages and disadvantages in relation to your own patients and your topic. If your patients' needs are very different, if they might find reading difficult or if

you will be describing complex procedures, then a leaflet may not
be the best way of providing information. You might want to
think about producing an audio or video tape instead.

What are the aims of your leaflet?

It is important to work out exactly what you want your leaflet to
achieve. Being clear about your aims will help you choose what
information to include. It will also help you when you come to
evaluate your leaflet (see Chapter 7).

Your aims might include some of the following:

• to increase knowledge and understanding;

• to correct misunderstandings;

• to reduce anxiety;

• to raise awareness about a service;

• to give instructions, for example about how to use an inhaler.

Bear in mind the limitations of leaflets when you work out your
aims. Be realistic, especially about changing your patients'
attitudes and behaviour. Many things influence our attitudes and
the way we behave, and having accurate information is only one
of them. For example, a teenager who has diabetes may
understand how to manage his or her diet, but being able to do
what their friends do may be a much more important concern.

Also, your leaflet may raise awareness of a service, but whether
your patients will use it may depend on many things, such as how
important this is in comparison with other demands on their time

What information should you include in your leaflet?

Most of the information you will want to include will be factual
information about your topic. However, your leaflet will be more
useful if it also acknowledges what it feels like to be a patient.
These are 4 steps you can take to help you find appropriate factual
information to include.

1. The most important step is to consult your patients themselves to find out what they know already and what else they need to know. Listening to the way they describe the information they need and the words they use will also help you to write clearly (see Chapter 3).

2. Consult other people too, for example your patients' families, former patients, health professionals with knowledge of your topic and specialist organisations.

3. Review the relevant literature about your topic, including articles and books, to make sure the information you are using is up to date. You can get journal articles and books from your local health promotion department or from the library at the Health Promotion Library Scotland (address and phone number on page 59).

4. Look at the leaflets other people have produced and identify their shortfalls and good points. For example, do they cover what happens in your hospital? Are they appropriate for your patients? Do you like them? If not, why not? Are there things you do like? If so, could you do something similar? When you consult your patients, you should ask them what they think of other people's leaflets too. They will be able to tell you what is useful to them and what is less useful.

If you want to take information directly from other leaflets you must make sure that you have permission from the organisations who produced them. Also, remember to acknowledge the source of any quotations or illustrations you use in your leaflet.

How will you distribute your leaflet?

You should decide early on how you will distribute your leaflet so you can make sure it reaches the patients you are writing it for. For example, a leaflet could be:

• placed on a table in the waiting area;

• displayed in a leaflet rack;

• handed out by a nurse or other health care professional;

• sent out routinely or in response to requests.

If other people are going to hand out the leaflet you need to involve them in the planning. Make sure they know exactly who the leaflet is for, what is in it and when to hand it out.

How much will your leaflet cost?

If you can use a word processor, or have a colleague who could do this for you, the information in the next chapters will help you to do most of the work involved in producing your leaflet yourself. This will keep financial costs down. However, one of the main costs involved in producing a leaflet is the time it takes. Before you begin, make sure you will have enough time to carry out all the stages we describe in the next chapters.

Another option is to employ other people to help produce your leaflet. If so, the information in this book will help you to brief them about what you want. The things you may want to pay for are:

• design, including illustrations;

• printing;

• research to pilot and evaluate the leaflet.

Your local health promotion department may be able to suggest suitable individuals or companies to help with these. You could also look in Yellow Pages under 'Designers', 'Printers & lithographers' and 'Market research & analysis'.

The cost of **design** work will depend on the length of your leaflet and how simple or elaborate it is. A longer leaflet in colour with several illustrations will cost more than a short, black and white leaflet with no illustrations. Costs also vary between different design companies. In general, large design and advertising agencies charge high fees. Freelance designers and small companies are usually less expensive.

To find out exactly what you will be charged for design work, you should send a brief to 2 or more designers and ask for a quotation.

You will find information about how to brief a designer at the end of Chapter 5 (page 27).

The cost of **printing** will also depend on the length of your leaflet and how simple or elaborate it is. In addition, the number of copies you print is a major factor. Unless the information in your leaflet is likely to change quickly, it is better to print in bulk because this reduces the cost of each leaflet. For example, if you print 1,000 copies, the cost of each leaflet may work out at, say, 8p a copy. But if you print 10,000 copies, each copy may only cost 2p. It is cheaper in the long run to print a few more copies than you need. If you have to reprint your leaflet because you have run out, this will be much more expensive.

As with design work, you should get quotations from 2 or more printers to find out exact costs. Information on how to get a quotation is included at the end of Chapter 5 (page 28).

The cost of **research** to pilot and evaluate your leaflet will depend on:

• the number and kind of questions you want to ask;

• how far the researchers will have to travel to do the work;

• how many people's opinions you want them to get;

• the methods you want to use.

To find out exact costs, you should send a brief covering this information to 2 or more researchers and ask them to tender for the work. The last 3 chapters of this book will help you to do this. At the end of Chapter 8 you will find a guide to the amount you might expect to pay for different kinds of research (page 51). You should remember that this was written in 1994, and costs may have increased since then.

Organising your information

Introduction

It is important to organise your leaflet so it makes sense to your patients and is easy to follow. In this chapter we look at some ways of doing this. These include:

• prioritising your information;

• ordering it appropriately;

• using headings;

• using numbers and bullet points.

As well as using this chapter as a guide, it is a good idea to consult people who have experience in producing health education leaflets. Your local health promotion department may be able to help.

Prioritising your information

You may have found a lot of information about your topic by asking people what they think is needed and by looking at relevant literature. Now you need to decide what you should include in your leaflet and what you should leave out. It is no use giving your patients so much information that they can't take any of it in.

A good way of prioritising is to start by listing all the information you have found. Then divide it into information you think is essential, useful and unnecessary. The main body of the leaflet should give only the most essential information. If you think other information is less essential but would be useful, for example a list of contact addresses, put it in a separate section or appendix.

Ordering information

The order in which you present your information can make a big difference in helping your patients to understand it. A useful rule of thumb is always to put the information considered most important by your patients first. For example, if your patients are worried about what is going to happen to them during a procedure, they won't take in information about why the procedure is necessary. You need to describe what will happen to them first. Another useful rule, if you are explaining a procedure, is always to present the information in the order it will happen if your patient is doing or experiencing it.

Using headings

Organising your information under headings will help your patients to find their way around it without getting lost. Your headings will be most useful if you make them informative and relevant to your patients rather than just descriptive. One way of doing this is to describe what it is you want your patients to be able to do when they've read that section of your leaflet. For example, 'Causes of depression' is not a good heading; it is too general. 'Understanding depression' is better because it tells me, the reader, what the information will help me to do.

Another way is to use a question and answer format. In this case, you might include information about the causes of depression under the heading 'What causes depression?' In a longer leaflet you may want to ring the changes by using a mixture of both kinds of heading.

If you have a lot of information to include under one heading it may be better to divide it under sub-headings. For example, a recent leaflet for people with dementia has a section on 'Planning for the future'. The information under this main heading is divided under sub-headings such as 'Work', 'Driving' and 'Living arrangements' to make it easier to follow.

As with main headings, you could also use a question and answer format for sub-headings, for example 'Will I be able to continue working?' and 'Can I go on driving?'

Using numbers and bullet points

When you are making several points under one heading or sub-heading, it can help your patients to follow them if you number them. Don't use Roman numbers (I, II, III or i, ii, iii, etc.) as they are harder to follow.

You can also use bullet points to help your patients follow your information. These are most effective where the points you are making are no more than a sentence each. For example, we have used bullet points at the beginning of each chapter to highlight what we are going to cover in the chapter.

Writing your leaflet

Introduction

The way in which you write your leaflet will make a crucial difference to whether your patients understand it and find it acceptable. In this chapter we look at how you can make sure your leaflet is well written by:

• presenting information simply;

• writing clearly;

• choosing your words thoughtfully.

Presenting information simply

You can help your patients to understand your information by:

• including only 1 main idea in each paragraph;

• making the first sentence of each paragraph the one which clearly identifies the main idea;

• using short, simple sentences to convey no more than 2 pieces of information at a time;

• emphasising and repeating your main points - never hiding them among less important points.

If your leaflet is going to be longer than 2 or 3 pages, a table of contents would be helpful. A summary of the most important information, in point form, at the beginning or end is also helpful.

Writing clearly

A clear, simple writing style is essential if your patients are to understand what you are saying. Listed below are 10 principles to guide you in writing clearly.

1. Use mainly short sentences, but bear in mind that a string of short sentences is 'bitty' and can be difficult to read. Some longer sentences, but not too many, will help your text to flow well.

2. When you are using sentences that have 2 clauses linked by 'because' or 'if', put the 'because' or 'if' clause first. For example, it is better to write 'If your wound starts to bleed, contact your doctor' than 'Contact your doctor if your wound starts to bleed'.

3. Whenever possible you should use ordinary words instead of specialised medical terms. However, at times it may be better to use a specialised term, for instance if you would lose the correct medical meaning by using an ordinary word. Also, if patients are familiar with some of the medical terms they will hear health workers using, they will be more able to communicate with them.

4. When you need to use a specialised word, explain what it means when you first use it. For example: 'Your breast X-ray, often called a mammogram, will only take a few minutes'. Alternatively, you could put a list of definitions at the front of your leaflet where your patients can find it easily.

5. Avoid using shortened forms of names such as acronyms and abbreviations - your patients may have no idea what they mean. If you think it is necessary to use a shortened term, explain what it stands for when you first use it. For example: 'The Special Care Baby Unit, or SCBU for short, is on the 2nd floor of the hospital'.

6. Use personal pronouns (I, we, us, you) rather than impersonal ones (they, he, she, one). Personal pronouns will help your patients to feel you are speaking to them.

7. Write as you would speak, rather than in an 'academic' style. A common 'academic' way of writing is to use passive verbs rather than active verbs. For example, if you write 'The tablets should be taken twice a day' you are using a passive verb. If you write 'Take the tablets twice a day' you are using an active verb. Active verbs make information easier to understand.

8. Always describe what you want people to do, not what you don't want them to do. For example, 'Give only when the patient wheezes' is clearer than 'Do not give unless the patient is wheezing'.

9. If you need to use numbers in your text it is better to use the figure rather than the full word. For example, write 'Take 2 tablets 3 times a day', rather than 'Take two tablets three times a day'.

10. Finally, check your leaflet for spelling or typing mistakes. If you are using a word processor, it may include a spelling checker to help with this. It is a good idea to ask someone else to read through the leaflet and check for mistakes too. It is easy to miss them yourself, and spelling checkers don't pick up everything.

Choosing words thoughtfully

The words you use in your leaflet should be relevant and acceptable to everyone who might read it, so it is important to choose them carefully.

Using only masculine words, like he, him, his, man or mankind, will make your leaflet less acceptable to women. Use both masculine and feminine words (his or her, she or he) or words that include both men and women (people, human beings) instead.

Terms which suggest that people from a particular group are all the same can be offensive. Don't use terms like 'the disabled', 'blacks', 'the elderly', etc. Use terms which recognise people as individuals. 'Disabled people' or 'people with disabilities', 'black people' and 'older people' are more acceptable.

Don't assume that all your patients are in the same situation. For example, if you use the words husband and wife, this assumes that all your patients are heterosexual and married. The word partner is better, because it is acceptable to gay and lesbian people and to both married and unmarried heterosexual couples.

Sometimes people disagree about what is acceptable. You should check whether or not the terms you have used are acceptable to your patients when you pilot your leaflet (see Chapter 6).

Testing for readability

Introduction

The information in the previous 3 chapters is intended to help you make your leaflet easier to read. A readability test is one way of finding out if you have achieved this. The main reason for using one of these tests is that the average reading age of adults in the UK is about 9 to 10 years, so it is important to keep leaflets straightforward. Although readability tests can help you with this they can have drawbacks, so you should always pilot your leaflet too.

In this chapter we look at:

• 2 tests for calculating readability;

• the potential drawbacks of readability tests.

Calculating readability

There are several ways of calculating readability using simple mathematical formulae. Most of the tests work by counting the number of long words and long sentences and relating this to the reading age necessary to understand the material.

Your local health promotion department may be able to carry out a computerised readability test for you. If you want to do your own test, the **Gunning Fog Index** is very easy. This is what you do:

1. Choose a 100 word sample of text from your leaflet;
   Count the total number of complete sentences in the sample;
   Count the total number of words in these sentences;
   Divide the number of words by the number of sentences. This

gives the average sentence length.

2. Now count the number of words with 3 or more syllables in the 100 word sample. For the purposes of the test, syllables are counted as the words sound rather than as they are written. So 'advised' is 2 syllables; 'applying' is 3. You should count numbers and symbols as less than 3 syllables and hyphenated words as 2 words.

3. Add the average sentence length to the total number of words with 3 or more syllables and multiply the result by 0.4. This gives you the Fog reading score.

4. Finally, add 5 to the Fog reading score to get the reading age necessary to understand your leaflet.

Another test you may come across is the **Flesch test**. This is more widely used than the Fog test, but it is not as easy to do yourself. Also, it can only identify material suitable for people with reading ages of 9 years and above, so it is better for testing leaflets for adults than for young children. The test uses a formula based on the average number of syllables in a word and the average number of words in a sentence. The result is called a 'reading ease' score.

If you do want to carry out your own Flesch test, some of the books and articles in the section on further reading at the end will tell you how to do it.

Some word processors include a grammar and style checker. These use 1 or more readability tests. As well as checking readability, they are useful for identifying long sentences, errors in punctuation and passive verbs.

Possible drawbacks of readability tests
Readability tests have some possible drawbacks. The following are the main ones.

1. Most readability tests were developed for use with educational materials for children. They were not intended for assessing health related materials for adults, and their accuracy in

assessing materials for people from different backgrounds has
not been checked.

2. The tests cannot take account of the 'people factor' involved in
   reading. In other words, they ignore things that may enable
   people to cope better or less well with a leaflet than tests would
   suggest. For example, your patients' motivation and interest, as
   well as their previous knowledge and experience, can make a
   difference to how easy they find your leaflet. Gender, cultural
   background and age can also make a difference.

3. Because they rely only on checking sentence and word length,
   readability tests ignore many of the design factors that might
   balance out the use of some longer words and sentences. For
   example, the ideas presented, the order of their presentation and
   the use of illustrations to explain ideas can all affect how easy
   a leaflet is to read.

4. Readability tests are only rough measures, accurate to within
   a certain range. They are less accurate when used on shorter
   documents, and they do not take into account that the shortest
   word may not be the most accurate. Also, they cannot check
   whether or not you have used words correctly.

These drawbacks mean that a leaflet which has a good readability
score may still not be easy to understand. So mathematically
measuring readability is no substitute for paying attention to the
way you organise, write and design your leaflet. Nor is it a
substitute for finding out what your patients think of your leaflet
by piloting it before you produce it in bulk.

Even so, readability tests are a useful first step to finding out
whether your leaflet is suitable for your patients. Using one may
reduce the amount of revision you need to do after piloting.

Designing your leaflet

Introduction

The way you design your leaflet is as important in helping your patients to read and understand it as how you organise and write it. In this chapter we explain some of the things you can do to make sure your leaflet's design is appropriate. These include:

• choosing the page size;

• choosing the best size and style of type;

• making your headings stand out;

• choosing the best line length;

• positioning your text on the page;

• formatting your text;

• using colour and illustrations;

• designing the cover for your leaflet.

We have assumed here that either you or a colleague will produce the leaflet on a word processor, because this is how many leaflets are produced these days. If you do produce the leaflet yourself, your local health promotion department may employ a graphic designer who could give you further advice.

However, you may decide to pay someone to design your leaflet for you. If so, the information in this chapter will help you to brief them about what you want. The last section in the chapter gives some advice about how to do this. Advice about briefing printers is also included.

Choosing the page size

Before you make any other decisions about the design of your leaflet you need to choose which size of page to use. This is because some of the decisions you make will be influenced by the size of your pages. These are 4 things you need to think about in choosing the best page size.

1. Where will your patients read your leaflet? If you want them to take the leaflet home, it needs to be small enough to slip into a pocket or carry in a bag. It also needs to be a size they can handle and read in comfort.

2. How will the leaflet be distributed? If the leaflet is going to be displayed on a rack you need to make sure it is big enough to be visible but small enough to fit the rack. If it is going to be posted out, you need to bear in mind that the cost of postage and envelopes may be higher if you choose a larger size.

3. How much information do you have to include? If you have a lot of information, choosing a smaller page size may make your leaflet too bulky to read comfortably.

4. What size of type and line length is best for your patients? We discuss these later in this chapter. However, it is important to note here that your page size should allow you to use a large enough size of type without cramming the words on the page or having too few words on each line.

Although it is possible to produce leaflets in many different page sizes, most people choose 1 of 3 sizes. These are some are some of their advantages and disadvantages, starting with the largest size.

An **A4 page** is the same size as the paper most commonly used in photocopiers and computer printers. The main advantages of A4 pages are that you can include a lot of information without your leaflet becoming bulky, and it is easy to use larger type sizes. The disadvantages are that your leaflet will not be easy to carry without folding it, and an A4 leaflet is more difficult to read comfortably than a smaller leaflet.

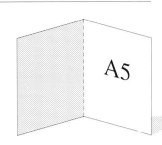

An **A5 page** is the size of an A4 sheet of paper folded in half along its width. You can still include a lot of information and use larger type sizes in an A5 leaflet, but it will be easier to carry and handle than A4. The main disadvantage is that your leaflet will still be too large to slip into a pocket.

A **1/3 A4 page** is the size of an A4 sheet of paper folded in 3 along its width. These leaflets have the advantage that they will fit into a standard office envelope, which makes them economical to post. They are also easy to slip into a pocket so your patients will have no problem taking your leaflet home to read. Their main disadvantage is that it is not easy to use larger type sizes without ending up with too few words on each line.

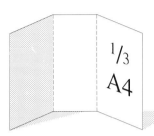

Choosing the best size of type

It is important to use type that is large enough for your patients to read. Word processors offer a range of type sizes. These are called 'point' sizes. The best size for general readers is 12 point type, but older people, other people who don't see well and children need a larger size.

This is 10 point type – too small for most readers.

This is 12 point type – the Royal National Institute for the Blind uses this point size in leaflets for general readers. We have used it for this book.

This is 14 point type – commonly used in large print books.

This is 16 point type – the Royal National Institute for the Blind sometimes uses 16 point in leaflets for partially sighted people.

While you need to make sure the type you choose is large enough for all your patients, bear in mind that some people may feel they are being treated like children if the type is too large.

Choosing the best style of type

As well as offering different sizes of type, word processors offer a choice of type styles (called fonts). There are 3 things to consider in deciding which font to use for your leaflet.

1. Some fonts are bigger and therefore easier to read than others, regardless of what size of type you use. For example, 'Times New Roman', which we have used for this book, is a medium-sized font.

   But this sentence is typed in 'Times' which is smaller, even though it is the same size of font (12 point) as the rest of the book.

   And this sentence is in 'Bookman', which is a larger font, but still 12 point.

   The most important thing is to choose a font which is large enough for your patients.

A serif letter.

2. You need to decide whether to use a 'serif' or 'sans serif' font. If you use a serif font, this means the individual letters you type will have fine finishing strokes at the top and bottom - a bit like curly tops and tails. 'Times New Roman' and 'Times' are both serif fonts.

   If you use a sans serif font, the letters you type won't have the curly tops and tails (sans is the French for without). This makes them look squarer than a serif font.

This sentence is typed in 'Helvetica', which is a sans serif font.

The kind of font you use can make a difference to your patients. The advantage of serif fonts is that the curly tops and tails help the reader's eye to scan across the page, and that helps them to grasp the content of what they're reading more quickly.

On the other hand, people with visual impairments may find sans serif fonts easier to read because the individual letters are easier to distinguish from each other. So choosing which to use is partly a matter of what you think looks best for your leaflet, but you also need to think carefully about which will be best for your patients.

A sans serif letter

3. Some fonts, like 'Times', have an academic look which may not be appropriate for a patient education leaflet. Others, like 'Courier' and 'Monaco' make leaflets look as if they've been produced on an ordinary typewriter, which these days can mean they look unprofessional.

```
This sentence is typed in 'Monaco'
```

It is a good idea to try out some fonts to see how they look before you decide which one to use.

Choosing the best line length

Most word processors allow you to choose how wide the margins at the side of each page of your leaflet will be. If you choose narrow margins on a large page size you will end up with more characters on each line, and that will make your leaflet harder to read. (Characters include numbers, punctuation marks and spaces as well as letters.)

On the other hand, if you choose wide margins on a small page size or with a large type size, you will only be able to fit a few words on each line. This will also make your leaflet harder to read, because people need to be able to scan enough words at a time for the information to make sense.

For A4 size pages, a common margin width is 1.25 inches. Using 12 point type, this means you end up with between 60 and 70 characters on each line, which is the maximum most writers recommend.

If you decide to use A5 pages, 1 inch margins are better. Using 12 point type, this will give you about 50 characters on each line.

If you are using 1/3 A4 pages, you will need smaller margins. Most people use 1/2 inch margins at each side. With 12 point type, this will give you about 40 characters on each line.

Whichever page size you use, don't be tempted to split words at the end of a line to fit more in. This will make your leaflet more difficult to read.

Making your headings stand out

You can make headings stand out by leaving plenty of empty space around them, by making them bold or by using a larger size of type. We have tried to make the headings in this book stand out by leaving plenty of space around them, and by making them bold. Whichever way you choose, be consistent throughout your leaflet. This will help your patients to find their way around the leaflet easily.

If you need to use sub-headings as well as main headings you can make it clear which is which by leaving less empty space around the sub-headings, or by using a larger size of type for the main headings. Again, it is important to be consistent throughout your leaflet.

Don't use capital letters to make your headings stand out. Headings entirely in capitals are not easy to read because you have to look at each individual letter rather than scanning a whole word at a time. Only use capitals at the beginning of a sentence, for the first letter of proper names and for acronyms and abbreviations.

Underlining can also make headings difficult to read because it blurs the distinction between letters:

Living with diabetes

Positioning your text on the page

When you type on a word processor, it automatically starts each line at the left hand margin. This makes a neat, even line down the left side of the page, sometimes called 'ranged left' text. You can also position text in 3 other ways.

1. You can have the word processor finish each line right up against the right hand margin, making a neat, even line down that side of the page too. This is known as 'justified' text. Although it looks nice and neat, justified text can be harder to read. This is because in order to fill each line completely the word processor leaves uneven spaces between each word, so the reader can't scan the text as quickly.

2. You can place text in the centre of the page rather than starting from the left hand margin. This can be useful, for example in creating title pages. But using centred text in the main body of a leaflet can make it harder to read. For this reason it is better not to place headings in the centre of the page either. Start them at the left hand margin like the rest of your text and your leaflet will be easier to read.

3. As well as choosing the position of the main text of your leaflet, you can choose where to position page numbers. If your leaflet is more than 2 or 3 pages long, page numbers will help your patients find their way around the information. The best place for them is at the outside corner of each page, where they are easy to find. We've positioned our page numbers in the top corner of the page, but you could have them in the bottom corner instead.

Formatting your text

We've already mentioned that you can make your headings stand out by printing them in bold. We've also mentioned that underlining words makes them harder to read because it blurs the distinction between letters. Printing words in bold and underlining them are 2 ways of formatting text. Another way is to print words in italic, *like this*.

Although formatting is useful for making headings stand out and for giving extra emphasis to key words, you should use it sparingly. Too much formatting distracts and confuses the reader.

Ranged left text

Justified text

Centred text

We've used a *lot* of formatting in this paragraph so **you** can see for yourself. There's *italic* for *emphasis*, **bold** to **grab** your attention and even some <u>underlining</u> for <u>extra</u> emphasis. We think by the time you've read to the *end* of the paragraph you'll be **really** distracted, even *irritated* by it.

Using colour

In deciding whether or not to use colour in your leaflet, you need to think about:

• making your leaflet easy to read;

• the cost involved if you are going to pay for printing;

• how the leaflet will look.

If you are going to employ a printer, the least expensive option is to use only black print. If you do this, you can make your leaflet more colourful by having it printed on coloured paper. However, it is important to have a contrast between the background paper and the print so the print shows up easily. Black print on a cream or white background is easiest to read. If you want to use coloured paper, choose very pale shades.

The most expensive option is to use full colour. This means using 3 other colours as well as black. However, you don't need to use full colour to achieve a colourful effect. You can use 1 or 2 other colours in different shades. You can also combine 2 colours to create a new colour without adding to the cost.

It is important to be sensitive in selecting colours to ensure that they are in keeping with your subject and the tone of your leaflet. For instance, many people find red an angry colour.

Word processors with a colour printer allow you to mix lots of colours or shades on the same page, but this will distract and confuse your readers. Use colour to make your leaflet attractive, but don't get carried away.

If possible, ask your patients what they think of the colours you've used when the leaflet is being piloted. If you can't produce a colour copy of your leaflet before piloting it, show your patients examples of the colours you are thinking of using.

Using illustrations

Illustrations can be a useful way of explaining something and showing positive images of your patient group. However, they can also distract people from the information you are trying to get across, so don't use them simply because they are pretty or use up space. If you are planning to use illustrations, here are some things to aim for:

1. Keep your illustrations as simple as possible. The most useful illustrations contain a single idea with a minimum of clutter. Simple, labelled line drawings are more effective than illustrations with lots of background shading and too much labelling.

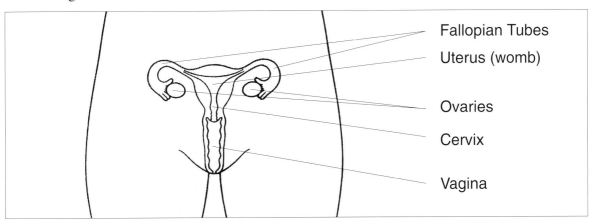

Fallopian Tubes

Uterus (womb)

Ovaries

Cervix

Vagina

2. Make sure your illustration is visible. It should be big enough to attract attention, not hidden away in a corner of the page. The lines used in the illustration should be heavy enough to be seen clearly. The type size you use for labelling and captions should also be large enough for your patients. Remember that illustrations for older people and other people who don't see well will need to be larger and even less cluttered.

3. Make sure your illustration makes sense to your patients. Place it next to or underneath the text to which it refers, so they can look easily at both. If you are illustrating part of the body, make sure you show enough of the body around the part you are illustrating for your patients to recognise it.

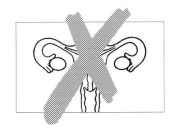

4. Don't use symbols without explaining what they mean. For example, you may know that ♀ means female and ♂ means male, but your patients may not.

Here are some things to avoid:

1. Don't position your text around an illustration - this will make the text difficult to follow.

2. Don't exclude anyone. If your illustration shows people, make sure it represents all your patients, for example by including men, women, people from different ethnic backgrounds and people of different ages. This applies to line drawings too.

3. Don't use cartoons to illustrate something that may be a serious matter for your patients. Humour can be a good way of putting information across, but it can be offensive when used in the wrong place.

4. Don't alarm your patients. Depending on what you are illustrating, too much realistic detail and use of colour may be frightening. You need to find a balance between being realistic enough for your patients to recognise what you are illustrating and alarming them. This is another reason simple, labelled line drawings are often best.

Designing your cover

First impressions are important, so the cover of your leaflet should make your patients want to pick it up. Also, the title should be short and give a clear idea of what the leaflet is about. The most helpful title is one which is informative and relevant to your patients. For example 'Diabetes' is not a good title because it is too general. 'What is diabetes?' is better because it gives people a more specific idea of what you are going to tell them. But 'Living with diabetes' is better still because it is applicable to me, the reader.

You should be careful that your title doesn't alarm your patients. Again, piloting will help you with this. For example, a leaflet which was produced for women invited for treatment after a smear test was originally called 'Your abnormal smear result'. However, piloting showed that this was alarming, and the title was changed to 'The result of your smear'.

Using a logo on the cover can bring together a range of different leaflets and create a sense of identity and ownership. For example, you may want to use a logo to link several leaflets on the same condition, or to link all the leaflets produced by your organisation.

It is a good idea to include the month and year when the leaflet was produced on the front or back cover. This will let other people know how up to date the information is. It will also remind you to check and update your leaflet (see 'Reviewing your leaflet' at the end of Chapter 7).

Briefing designers and printers

Before you contact **designers** to ask about their fees you should prepare a draft brief so you can talk through what you want on the phone. If the people you contact are interested in giving you a quotation, you can then send them the brief with any further information they have asked for. (See page 5 for information about how to find designers in your area.)

When you are preparing your brief, it is helpful to write a general introduction first, explaining as much as possible about your leaflet, for example:

• the subject and aim of the leaflet;

• who it is intended for;

• the length of the leaflet;

• your total budget.

Your brief should then give more detailed information about the issues covered in this chapter, including:

• the size of page you want to use;

• the size and style of type you want to use;

• the positioning of text on the page;

• how many different sorts of headings and subheadings your
leaflet includes;

• how many colours you want to use;

• a description of any illustrations you want to include.

Once you have accepted a quotation, you should meet with the
designer to talk through your brief again. It is important to be sure
that he or she understands exactly what you want.

To get quotations from **printers**, you will need to provide
information about:

• the length of your leaflet;

• how many colours you want to use;

• how many copies you want;

• your budget for printing.

To work out how many copies to print, you need to decide how
long you want your supply of leaflets to last. For example, if you
include information like contact names which may change quickly
you will not want a supply of leaflets which will last for years.

Once you have decided how long you want your supply to last,
you should estimate how many copies you will need to distribute
each month. This will give you an idea of the total number of
copies you need. Bear in mind that you may want to distribute
more copies in the first month or so.

The quality of paper you use will also affect the cost of printing.
The printers you contact will be able to tell what is available
within your budget once they know more about your leaflet and
how many copies you need. The most important thing is that the
paper should not be so thin that the print shows through on the
other side.

Piloting

Introduction

Piloting your leaflet involves asking your patients for their views about your leaflet. This is sometimes called pre-testing. It is crucial to carry out a pilot before you produce the leaflet in its final form. This will enable you to answer 4 important questions:

• whether your patients find the leaflet interesting enough to pick up;

• whether they understand it;

• whether you have included the most useful information;

• whether your patients believe it.

Before you pilot your leaflet with your patients, it is important to make sure the information in it is accurate. You should check this first with specialists in your topic area.

When you are piloting your leaflet, you may need to encourage your patients to say what they really think. Patients are often so grateful for a service that they are unwilling to make any criticisms. When they do offer criticism, you need to be prepared to accept it and make any changes suggested. If a lot of revisions are needed, you should pilot the revised leaflet again.

Patients may be happier to say what they think to someone who wasn't involved in producing a leaflet, so you might prefer to ask colleagues to help with your pilot. Alternatively, if your budget will allow it, you could employ outside researchers. (See page

51) for information about costs.)

In case neither of these options is possible we have written this chapter as though you will carry out your pilot yourself. However, the information here will also help you to brief a colleague or outside researchers. We look at 3 things:

• the ethical issues you need to think about;

• the different ways in which you can ask questions;

• how to decide who to ask.

Because the methods you can use to pilot your leaflet can also be used to evaluate it, we describe these separately in Chapter 8.

The books listed in the section on further reading under 'Piloting and evaluation' will give you further advice about carrying out a pilot. Your local health promotion department may be able to help too.

Ethical issues

When you approach patients to ask for their views you need to be honest about how confidential and anonymous the information they give you will be. They have the right to this information before making up their minds about whether or not they want to help you.

Confidential information is information that is only ever known to the person who gives it and the person or people to whom they give it.

You should only promise complete confidentiality if you are sure no one else will ever receive the information. If you are going to share the information with other people, either verbally or in a report, then you must tell the patients whose views you are seeking who will receive it.

Anonymous information is information from an unnamed source.

You should tell the patients you are asking to help you whether other people will know who they are, and if not how you will make sure they are anonymous. This will certainly involve leaving out or changing any personal names in a written or verbal report. It may also mean leaving out or changing the names of hospitals, clinics or geographical areas that might identify someone.

Asking questions

The questions you ask your patients about your leaflet should encourage them to express their views, whether positive or negative, as openly as possible. It is important simply to listen to their comments - don't be tempted to justify the way your leaflet is.

You will get more useful information by asking a mixture of open and closed questions.

Open questions are questions that allow people to answer in their own words. For example, if you ask 'What do you think of the cover?', you are asking an open question because the wording leaves your patients free to tell you what they like and dislike.

Open questions are useful when people might like some things but not others. They are also useful for finding out how your patients think you could improve your leaflet. Their disadvantage is that they invite lengthy answers, so you could end up with a lot of information to analyse.

Closed questions are questions that make people answer in a particular way. If you ask 'Is the cover eye-catching?', you are asking a closed question because your patients are likely to answer just 'yes' or 'no'. They will not feel as free to explain if there are some things they like about the cover and others they don't like.

But closed questions are useful when you need definite answers, for example about whether your patients have understood your leaflet. They also invite shorter answers that are easier to analyse.

When you are asking closed questions, try not to begin with 'Do you ...' or 'Does it ...'. Questions like this, such as 'Do you like the cover?' or 'Does the leaflet look interesting?', tend to prompt people to answer 'yes'.

Exactly how you will use open and closed questions will depend on the method you use (see Chapter 8). These are some suggestions you can adapt to whichever method you choose.

Some useful **open questions** might be:

• What do you think of the cover?

• If you only saw the cover, what would you say the leaflet was about?

• What do you think of the colours we've used?

• What do you think of the illustrations?

• How could we improve the leaflet?

• What sort of person would you say wrote the leaflet?

The last question is useful for finding out whether your patients feel your leaflet was written by someone who understands their situation.

Some useful **closed questions** might be:

• Is the cover too bright, too dull or about right?

• Would most patients understand the leaflet?

• Is all the information in the leaflet necessary?

• Is there anything else you would like to know?

• Are there any words in the leaflet which offend you?

• Is the print too small, too big, or about right?

• Are the illustrations clear?

• Would most patients understand what we've drawn in the illustrations?

• Is the leaflet too short, too long, or about right?

If you are using closed questions like the last one, which offer
people a choice of answers, you might want to print the answers
to choose from on a card. This will allow your patients to see
them as well as hear them. Cards like these are called
'showcards'.

> ## Is the leaflet:
> – too short?
> – too long?
> – about right?

Of course, you wouldn't ask all your open questions first and then
all your closed questions. For example, it would make sense to
find out everything your patients have to say about the cover
before going on to ask about the information in the leaflet. If
your leaflet is more than a few paragraphs long, it is a good idea
to go through it section by section asking about each section in
turn.

When you are using a mixture of open and closed questions, it is
often useful to ask an open question first (What do you think of
the cover?) to see what your patients have to say. Depending on
what they say, you can then ask some more specific closed
questions (Are the colours too light or too dark?).

Whichever kind of question you are using, make sure you only
ask about 1 thing at once. For example, if you ask 'What do you
think of the colour and design of the leaflet?' you are asking
about 2 separate things and you may not get clear answers about
both.

Deciding who to ask

Your patients are the most important people to ask about your
leaflet. If they are a small group, for example patients who have a
relatively rare condition, you may be able to include them all.

If more people are involved, you will need to choose a sample to represent the whole group. You can do this by selecting patients from a ready made list, for example a list of all the patients admitted to a ward over the last 6 months, or from a list you make up yourself.

It is important to make sure the patients you choose for your sample are not biased towards a particular group. You need to make sure they represent everyone your leaflet is written for.

If you just select the first 30 patients from a list, this could bias your sample. For example, if the list is alphabetical you may exclude Sikh men because their last name will be Singh, which will mean they are towards the end of the list. Or if patients are listed by where they live, you might miss those from a particular social class who tend to live in one of the areas listed last.

A better way to choose your sample is to take say every third or every tenth name from the list, depending how long it is and how many patients you are able to consult.

Make sure the way you choose your sample is ethical and legal. If you need to consult medical records to get a list of patients, you must have permission from your Local Research Ethics Committee. Bear in mind that this could take 2 to 3 months. If the list you are using is held on a computer, you must be registered to use this information under the Data Protection Act. Your local health promotion department should be able to provide further details about how to contact your Ethics Committee and about the Data Protection Act.

As well as the patients for whom your leaflet is written, other people may be able to give you valuable comments. For example, you may want to consult your patients' families and carers, or other staff who will use the leaflet with patients.

If you do decide to involve other people, you may find that their advice conflicts with your patients' opinions. Unless the advice concerns the accuracy of medical information, you should generally give priority to your patients' opinions. You are producing the leaflet for them, so their opinions are the most important.

Evaluation

7

Introduction

There is an important difference between piloting your leaflet and
evaluating it. Whereas the purpose of piloting is to find out
whether the patients your leaflet is written for find it attractive,
easy to understand and believable, the purpose of evaluation is to
find out whether the leaflet achieves what you want it to achieve.

In this chapter we look at:

• how you can work out your evaluation aims;

• how you can design your evaluation;

• how you can use the information you get;

• reviewing your leaflet once you have evaluated it.

Although the purpose of evaluation is different from piloting,
some of the things you need to think about are the same. You can
find information about the following in Chapter 6:

• the ethical issues involved (page 30);

• asking open and closed questions (page 31);

• deciding who to ask (page 33).

The methods you can use for evaluation are also the same as for
piloting. We describe these in the next chapter.

We have written this chapter as though you will be carrying out your evaluation yourself. However, as with piloting, your patients may be more comfortable saying what they think of your leaflet to someone who wasn't involved in producing it. You might want to ask colleagues to help you with this, or use outside researchers instead (see page 51 for approximate costs). Your local health promotion department may be able to offer further advice, and the books listed in the section on further reading will give you more information too.

Working out your evaluation aims

To work out the aims of your evaluation you need to return to the aims you identified for your leaflet itself. In Chapter 1 we suggested these might include some of the following:

• to increase knowledge and understanding;

• to correct misunderstandings;

• to reduce anxiety;

• to raise awareness about a service;

• to give instructions.

These aims are all to do with changing something: your patients' knowledge, their anxiety levels, their awareness, or their ability to do something practical like use an inhaler.

The aims of your evaluation will therefore be about finding out whether these changes have taken place. They may include some of the following:

• to discover whether your patients understand more about your topic;

• to find out whether they are less anxious after reading it;

• to assess whether patients are more aware of your service now;

• to find out whether your patients are more confident about carrying out a procedure.

Be realistic in setting your aims, especially about changing
behaviour (see page 3).

Designing your evaluation

Because evaluation involves finding out about changes, your
evaluation design needs to allow you to compare what your
patients knew, felt, were aware of or were able to do **before** they
read your leaflet and **after** they read it.

For this reason it is helpful to think about evaluation designs in
terms of 'before' and 'after'. Depending on your time and
budget, and how precise you need the results to be, you could use
an 'after only' evaluation design, or a 'before and after' design.

As you would expect, the **after only evaluation** involves asking
your patients for information only after they have read your
leaflet.

The advantage of this design is that it is relatively quick and
inexpensive. The disadvantage is that you are relying on what
your patients remember from before they read your leaflet, and on
what they tell you about its influence on them. It's easy to forget
how you felt or what you knew even a few hours ago. Also, some
patients might say your leaflet has had a positive influence
because they want to please you or because they don't want to
appear ignorant.

The **before and after evaluation** enables you to be more certain
about whether your leaflet has made a difference. If you use this
design you would ask questions about what your patients know or
feel or are confident about doing before they read your leaflet.
You would then ask them the same questions again after they've
read it and compare their answers to see if there's been any
change. It is best to leave some time between the 2 stages in case
having answered your questions at the before stage influences the
answers your patients give at the after stage.

Although the before and after design will provide you with more
precise information about whether your leaflet is achieving its

aims, it is more time consuming than the after only design. Also, of course, you are taking up twice as much of your patients' time. You might be able to minimise the time involved if you ask them to help with your evaluation when you are in contact with them anyway, for example when they are attending a clinic.

Using the information you get from your evaluation

As with piloting, you need to be open to criticism of your leaflet and willing to make any changes suggested by your evaluation.

If your leaflet has been piloted, it is unlikely that your findings will be totally negative. It is much more likely that they will suggest ways of making the leaflet more effective than it already is. In this case, you don't need to make immediate changes, but you should include any improvements suggested by the evaluation before the leaflet is reprinted.

If the evaluation shows that your leaflet is confusing or makes patients more anxious, you should withdraw it and decide whether or not to rewrite it.

As well as using the information you get from your evaluation to improve the leaflet itself, you may want to share it with other staff who might use the leaflet with their patients.

Reviewing your leaflet

The information in a leaflet can go out of date quickly, and fashions in design also change over time. For these reasons you should review your leaflet regularly after you have evaluated it.

To do this you need to keep up to date with current knowledge about your topic. It is also important to make sure any contact names, addresses and phone numbers you give are still correct. If the information in your leaflet becomes out of date, you should revise it as soon as possible.

It is a good idea to check with some of your patients that they still find the leaflet relevant. You could do this informally by asking your patients for comments when they have time to help you, for example when they are attending a clinic.

How often you need to revise your leaflet will depend on your topic and who the leaflet is intended for. Whatever interval you decide is best, it is a good idea to build a review into your planning cycle so you don't lose sight of the need to do this.

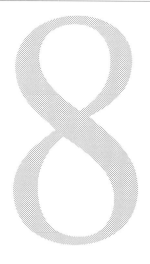

Choosing piloting and evaluation methods

Introduction

There is no perfect method for piloting and evaluating your leaflet. All the methods you can use have advantages and disadvantages that you need to consider. Which method you choose will also depend on who your leaflet is written for, and on your time and budget.

In this chapter we describe the 4 main piloting and evaluation methods:

• group interviews;

• semi-structured individual interviews;

• written questionnaires;

• structured interviews.

We look at the advantages and disadvantages of each of these methods and outline some of the things you need to think about if you decide to use them. Table 1 on page 50 summarises their main advantages. Table 2 on page 51 will give you an idea of what you might expect to pay outside researchers, depending on which method you choose. Bear in mind that costs may well have increased since we wrote this book.

Some of the information in Chapter 6 is relevant here too. You may want to refer to the section on confidentiality and anonymity (page 30) and the section on open and closed questions (page 31).

You will find more information in the books listed under 'piloting and evaluation' in the section on further reading. Your local health promotion department may also be able to help.

Group interviews

Group interviews are sometimes called focus group discussions. They are a popular piloting and evaluation method because they allow you to ask several people for their opinions at the same time.

Some other **advantages of group interviews** are:

• they can stimulate more discussion than individual interviews;

• they are relatively quick and inexpensive;

• you can ask open questions easily;

• your patients can ask you to explain your questions;

• you can ask them to explain their replies.

Some **disadvantages of group interviews** are:

• some topics may be too sensitive for group discussion;

• some people find it harder to say what they think in a group;

• people who feel different from the others, for example if they are disabled or from a different ethnic group, may feel unable to say what they think;

• group interviews may be too complicated if your leaflet is long;

• analysing people's replies can be time consuming;

• it may be difficult to bring your patients together in a group.

The ideal number of people to include in a group interview is 6 to 8. If you decide to use this method you may need to interview several groups to make sure that everyone your leaflet is intended for is represented.

You may also need to interview several groups to make sure people don't feel at a disadvantage or embarrassed. For example, women may feel more comfortable discussing some issues if there are no men in the group.

Before you begin each interview, you should explain how confidential and anonymous the information your patients give you will be. Make sure you have their agreement before you carry on with the interview.

You will need a checklist of topics you want to cover when you are conducting your interviews. You don't have to stick to it rigidly - it's better to let the conversation flow so long as it is relevant. However, it is easy to forget to ask important questions if you don't have a checklist.

You will also need to think about how to get a good record of the interview, because it is impossible to remember everything people say. It is very hard both to ask questions and to take notes. If possible, you should ask someone else to help you run the interviews. They should try to write down everything people say rather than just brief notes. It can be difficult to remember what brief notes mean, and your patients' own words can tell you a lot more.

An alternative is to use a tape recorder, but you must ask your patients' permission first. As long as they know how confidential and anonymous the information they give you will be, most people are willing to allow this.

Semi-structured individual interviews

Individual interviews are described as 'semi-structured' when they use a checklist of topics to cover rather than a set list of questions (see 'Structured interviews' later in this chapter). They are a useful alternative to group interviews if it is difficult for your patients to meet together.

Some other **advantages of semi-structured individual interviews** are:

• your patients may feel more comfortable discussing sensitive topics one to one;

• they are less complicated if your leaflet is long;

• you can ask open questions easily;

• your patients can ask you to explain your questions;

• you can ask them to explain their replies.

Some **disadvantages of semi-structured individual interviews** are:

• they are time consuming and relatively expensive;

• some patients may feel uncomfortable being the focus of all your attention;

• analysing people's replies can be time consuming.

If you decide to use this method, many of the things you will need to remember are the same as for group interviews:

• to make sure all the patients your leaflet is intended for are represented;

• to explain about confidentiality and anonymity and get your patients' permission to continue;

• to prepare a checklist of topics to cover so you don't forget anything;

• to get a good record of the interview.

Asking someone else to take notes during an individual interview is not a good idea, because the person being interviewed may feel overwhelmed by 2 people. This means you will need to take notes yourself or use a tape recorder. As with group interviews, you must ask permission before taping an interview.

Written questionnaires
These can be useful if it is too difficult or time consuming to carry out interviews.

Some other **advantages of written questionnaires** are:

• they are a relatively inexpensive way of getting a lot
  of people's opinions;

• they allow your patients to tell you what they
  think anonymously;

• people's replies are easy to analyse.

Some **disadvantages of written questionnaires** are:

• your patients may not fill them in, so you may
  not get many replies;

• the replies you do get may be biased, for example if only
  the patients who like your leaflet fill in their questionnaire;

• you need to ask mainly closed questions so your patients
  can reply easily;

• your patients may not understand your questions;

• they need to be able to read and write fairly well to fill
  in a questionnaire;

• designing a questionnaire can be time consuming.

The way you write and design your questionnaire can help you to
overcome some of these disadvantages. These are 6 steps you can
take:

1. Make sure your questionnaire is easy to read and understand.
   Use short words and sentences, clear print and plenty of space
   to separate your questions.

2. Remember to explain how confidential and anonymous your
   patients' replies will be, either on your questionnaire itself or
   in a letter enclosed with it.

3. Keep your questionnaire as short as possible. Too many
   questions can be daunting, and your patients are more likely to
   fill in a short questionnaire.

4. Decide how you want your patients to answer your questions

and be consistent throughout the questionnaire. For example, you could ask your patients to tick boxes beside the answers they choose. We've shown this method in most of the illustrations in this chapter. Alternatively, you could ask your patients to circle their answer, as in the illustration below. Don't ask your patients to do both in the same questionnaire as this is confusing.

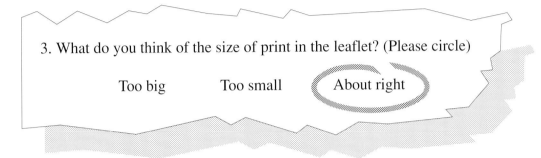

3. What do you think of the size of print in the leaflet? (Please circle)

        Too big   Too small   About right

5. Include clear instructions about how to fill in the questionnaire. It is a good idea to give an example of how to fill in the answer to 1 question so your patients can see what you want them to do.

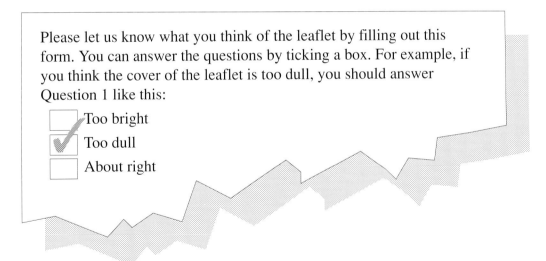

Please let us know what you think of the leaflet by filling out this form. You can answer the questions by ticking a box. For example, if you think the cover of the leaflet is too dull, you should answer Question 1 like this:

☐ Too bright
☑ Too dull
☐ About right

6. After you have written the questionnaire, try it out with a few of your patients to see whether they understand it. Make changes to the wording and design based on what they tell you.

Choosing the best format for your questions is also an important part of questionnaire design. There are 2 main kinds of closed questions you can ask:

• yes/no questions;

• multiple choice questions.

Yes/No questions simply ask people to answer 'yes' or 'no'. They are useful for asking straightforward questions, for example 'Would most patients understand the leaflet?'

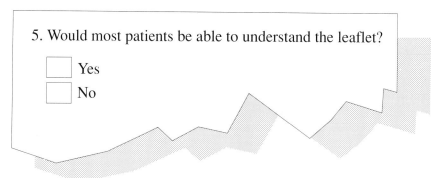

5. Would most patients be able to understand the leaflet?

   ☐ Yes

   ☐ No

Multiple choice questions can be asked in 2 ways. You can ask your patients to choose only 1 answer from a list of several, or you can ask them to tick as many answers as apply.

8. What do you think of the length of the leaflet?
   (Please tick one box)

   ☐ Too short

   ☐ Too long

   ☐ About right

9. Should the leaflet give more information about any of these? (please tick as many boxes as you want)

   ☐ The causes of diabetes

   ☐ How insulin works

   ☐ Managing your diet

   ☐ Taking exercise

   ☐ Drinking alcohol

Because closed questions like these make people answer in fixed ways, it is a good idea to include some open questions too. You could do this by asking your patients to explain their answers to some of your closed questions. Remember to leave enough space for people to reply. It is also a good idea to leave space at the end of the questionnaire for any other comments your patients may have.

10. Overall, how helpful did you find this leaflet?

☐ Very helpful

☐ Quite helpful

☐ Not very helpful

☐ Not at all helpful

Which parts of the leaflet did you find most helpful? (Please say why)

....

....

....

Which parts did you find least helpful? (Please say why)

....

....

....

11. Are there any other comments you would like to make about the lealfet?

....

....

....

Thank you for your help.

Once you have written and designed your questionnaire, you need to decide how to distribute it. You may be able to hand it out with your leaflet, or someone may be able to do this for you. Otherwise you will need to post it out to your patients, again with a copy of the leaflet.

If you are going to post out your questionnaire, you need to consider how your patients will feel when they receive it. It might make some patients anxious or upset to receive a questionnaire from a hospital or clinic. Also, you need to bear in mind that someone you send a questionnaire to may have died. Unless you are sure you will not upset or worry anyone, you should try to make contact in person first to check if sending the questionnaire is acceptable.

You will also need to consider how your patients are going to return the questionnaires. It may be possible to put a box somewhere for your patients to leave them. Otherwise you will need to enclose a reply paid envelope.

Structured interviews

These use similar questions to those you would ask in a written questionnaire. The difference is that you fill in the answers with your patients, rather than asking them to write in their own answers.

Some of the **advantages of structured interviews** are:

• you will get more replies than from written questionnaires;

• your patients don't need to be able to read and write;

• they are less time consuming than semi-structured interviews;

• people's replies are easy to analyse.

Some of the **disadvantages of structured interviews** are:

• they are more time consuming than written questionnaires;

• you need to ask mainly closed questions;

• your patients can't reply to you anonymously.

If you decide to use structured interviews many of the things you need to think about are the same as for written questionnaires. For example, the way you write and design your questionnaire will make a difference to how well your patients understand your questions, so the 6 steps listed earlier apply to this method too.

You can also use yes/no and multiple choice questions in the same way as you would in a written questionnaire. If you are using multiple choice questions, it may help to show your patients the answers to choose from printed on a card so they can see as well as hear them (see page 33).

As with written questionnaires, it is a good idea to ask some open questions too. Remember to leave yourself plenty of space on your questionnaire to write in your patients' answers. Try to write down everything they say rather than taking brief notes - it is easy to forget what notes mean a week later.

Table 1
Advantages of piloting and evaluation methods

	Group interviews	Individual interviews	Written questionnaires	Structured interviews
Relatively quick to design	X	X		
Relatively quick to carry out	X		X	X
Relatively quick to analyse			X	X
Easy to ask open questions	X	X		
Can explain questions and explore answers	X	X		
More people likely to respond	X	X		X

Table 2
Approximate research costs (1994 figures)

Method	Cost*
Group interview (6-8 People)	£800 – £1100 per group
Group interview (4-5 people)	£650 – £800 per group
Semi-structured interview	£150 – £300 per person
Structured individual interview	£25 – £35 for each person
Written questionnaire	£5 – £10 for each questionnaire

* The costs listed include collection and analysis of information, a verbal report and a final written report. Costs will vary within the range given, depending how long each interview is, how complex the analysis is and how much travelling is involved. Structured interview and questionnaire costs will also depend on the size of your sample.

Summary

In this book we have tried to give you a framework for producing a leaflet for your patients. We have included the main points to consider and suggested some ways you can make sure that your leaflet:

• is the best way to give information;

• includes information that you and your patients need and want;

• includes the most important information that you want to give;

• is likely to be read and understood by your patients;

• is reviewed and changed over time.

The book has been written to provide information and advice on producing leaflets for patients. We have not included information on writing for a wider audience, although many of the principles are the same. (Some useful references are included in the reading list which follows.)

You will get maximum benefit from this book if you also take part in training. This should be available through your local health promotion department.

We hope that you find the book a helpful reference guide.

Further reading

General information

Consumer leaflets - a write off?
written and published by Shire Hall Communications Ltd., London, in 1992.
The authors examined how easy 32 leaflets produced for the general public by the food, pharmaceutical and health care industries were to read and understand. They found that a third of the UK population would not be able to understand most of the leaflets. They also found that the print size of two thirds of the leaflets was too small. On the basis of these findings the authors make recommendations about how to develop more appropriate leaflets. A separate section on readability is included with a brief outline of several different tests.

Developing family information leaflets
by Alan Glasper and David Burge. Published in Nursing Standard, volume 6 (25), 1992, pages 24-27.
Offers guidance to staff working in paediatrics about producing family information leaflets.

The evaluation of patient education materials: focus on readability
by Patricia O'Laughlin Pasture and Barbara Kirsner Berg. Published in Patient Education and Counselling, volume 9 (2), 1987, pages 216-219.
Offers guidance to hospital staff on developing information leaflets. Based on the authors' own experience.

Guide lines: better information for hospital patients
by Roger Silver. Published by the King's Fund Centre, London in 1991.
An excellent guide to producing an introductory hospital information booklet for patients. Includes advice on how to brief printers or graphic designers. Also discusses the involvement of advertisers and the need for translations for minority ethnic groups.

How readable are practice leaflets?
by Tim Albert and Stephanie Chadwick. Published in the British Medical Journal, volume 305, 1992, pages 1266 - 1268.
Offers guidance on producing leaflets for use in general practice. Suggests 9 principles on which the development of leaflets should be based and describes how to use the Fog readability test.

Making health communication programmes work: a planner's guide
written by the United States Department of Health and Human Services. Published by the National Institute of Health in 1989 (publication number 89-1493).
A comprehensive guide to developing all types of health education materials and formats. Illustrated with plenty of examples, although their North American context means some will be more useful than others. Appendices contain detailed information about carrying out a readability test, along with sample questionnaires for use in piloting and evaluation.

Patient information leaflets - the state of the art
by J.B. Kitching. Published in the Journal of the Royal Society of Medicine, volume 83 (May), 1990, pages 298-300.
Although the author's main focus is on producing drug information leaflets, the advice is based on a wide ranging literature review and is relevant to other topics.

Please take a leaflet
by Mary Dixon. Published in Nursing, volume 5 (5), 1992, pages 11-13.
Offers guidance to nurses in compiling patient information leaflets.

The politics of health information
by Wendy Farrant and Jill Russell. Published by the Institute of Education, University of London in 1986.
Uses the production of a heart disease booklet as a case study to show how health messages can be distorted by emphasising individual change and ignoring the importance of the socio-economic environment for health status. Challenges some widely held beliefs about the information needs of the public and stresses the need for meaningful input from potential readers.

Design issues

Designing instructional text
written by James Hartley. Third edition published by Kogan Page in 1994.
Deals with a far wider range of written materials than patient education leaflets, but covers all the design issues you need to think about in producing a leaflet. Very technical in places, but written and designed in a way which makes it easy to read and understand.

Readability

How do they read you?
by Mike Church. Published by the Scottish Health Education Group in 1990.
An easy to read leaflet explaining readability tests. Describes how to use the Flesch test in detail. Provides a graph so you don't have to use the full formula, and a table for interpreting results. Available from the Health Promotion Library Scotland.

Readability formulas: cautions and criteria
by Cathy D. Meade and Cyrus F. Smith. Published in Patient Education and Counselling, volume 17, 1991, pages 153-158.
A comprehensive critique of readability tests, including grammar and style checkers.

Writing for your audience: is there a magic formula?
by Mary J. Breen. Published in Health Promotion,
Summer 1992, pages 2-6.
A comprehensive critique of readability tests.

Ethnic minority groups

Health in any language: a guide to producing health information for non-English-speaking people
edited by Sara Lovell. Published by the North East Thames Regional Health Authority, London in 1993.
Advice on how to develop appropriate messages in English and then translate them into other languages. Emphasises the importance of working with local community groups and fieldworkers who have close contact with ethnic minority groups.

Multilingual publications: some tips for first-time producers
by Keith Allan Noble. Published in Health Promotion,
Summer 1989, pages 6-7.
A short article providing general advice on developing leaflets for minority ethnic groups.

A strategy for information, health promotion and equal opportunities
written and published by the North Manchester Health Authority in 1991.
A pack containing guidelines for producing leaflets with examples in several languages, materials for a 2-day training course and a project report. Although some of the information is specific to North Manchester Health Authority, most of it is more widely applicable.

Illustrations

Effective use of patient education illustrations
by Linda Rohret and Kristi J. Ferguson. Published in Patient Education and Counselling, volume 15, 1990, pages 73-75.
Provides comprehensive guidance on designing illustrations. The authors selected 45 patient education leaflets containing at least 1 illustration. They then reviewed the relevant literature to develop a checklist for rating the leaflets.

People with visual impairments

The Royal National Institute for the Blind (RNIB) have established a campaign called 'See it Right' which aims to encourage information providers to produce material in a format which blind and partially sighted people can 'read'. Several publications are available, including these booklets:

Getting in touch with blind people:
a guide for information providers

See it right: new approaches
to information for blind and partially sighted people

A series of free factsheets is also available:

Clear print guidelines

How to produce Braille

An introduction to tape and large print methods

Copies of all these publications can be obtained from RNIB Public Policy Office, 224 Great Portland Street, London W1N 6AA, Tel 0171 388 1266. For technical advice about tape and Braille phone 0345 626271.

Piloting and evaluation

Consulting consumers:
A guide to good practice for the NHS in Scotland
written and published by the National Health Service in Scotland
and the Scottish Consumer Council in 1994.
A comprehensive guide which will help you with both piloting and evaluation. Provides advice about choosing a sample, designing a questionnaire, and using interviews. Gives examples from the NHS in Scotland. Also contains a list of Scottish-based researchers.

Evaluating health promotion: a health worker's guide
by Penelope Hawe, Deirdre Degeling and Jane Hall. Published by MacLennan and Petty in 1990.
Although not specifically about evaluating patient education leaflets, this book has useful sections on choosing a sample, designing a questionnaire, group interviews and evaluation designs. Don't be put off by its rather 'academic' appearance; it's quite easy to read.

Useful contacts

National Organisations

Patient Education Scotland
The Priory
Canaan lane
Edinburgh EH10 4SG
Tel. 0345 70 80 10

Health Promotion Library
Scotland
The Priory
Canaan lane
Edinburgh EH10 4SG
Tel. 0345 125 442

Local health promotion departments

Argyll & Clyde Health Board
Health Education Department
Ross House
Hawkhead Road
Paisley PA2 7BL
Tel. 0141 842 7255

Ayrshire & Arran Health
Board
Health Education Department
Ayrshire Central Hospital
Kilwinning Road
Irvine KA12 8SS
Tel. 01294 741919

Borders Health Board
Health Promotion Department
Huntlyburn House
Melrose TD6 9BP
Tel. 01896 754333

Dumfries & Galloway Health
Board
Health Education Department
Nithbank
Dumfries DG1 2SD
Tel. 01387 46246

Fife Healthcare NHS Trust
Health Promotion Department
Glenrothes House
North Street
Glenrothes KY7 5PB
Tel. 01592 754355

Forth Valley Health Board
Health Education Department
32 Spittal Street
Stirling FK7 7PX
Tel. 01786 450010

Grampian Health Board
Grampian Health Promotion
Dept.
1 Albyn Place
Aberdeen AB9 1RE
Tel. 01224 589901

Greater Glasgow Health
Board
Health Promotion Department
225 Bath Street
Glasgow G2 4JT
Tel. 0141 248 7644

Highland Health Board
Health Education Department
Royal Northern Infirmary
Ness Walk
Inverness IV3 5SS
Tel. 01463 704000

Lanarkshire Health Board
Health Education Department
Strathclyde Hospital
Airbles Road
Motherwell ML1 3BW
Tel. 01698 258800

Lothian Health Board
Health Promotion Department
61 Grange Loan
Edinburgh EH9 2EP
Tel. 0131 662 4661

Orkney Health Board
Balfour Hospital
New Scapa Road
Kirkwall KW15 1BY
Tel. 01856 872763

Shetland Health Board
Health Education Department
Brevik House, South Road
Lerwick ZE1 0RB
Tel. 01595 6767

Tayside Health Board
Health Education Department
7 Dudhope Terrace
Dundee DD3 6HG
Tel. 01382 28213

Western Isles Health Board
Health Education Department
37 South Beech Street
Stornoway
Isle of Lewis PA78 2BN
Tel. 01851 702997

Index

NOTES

NOTES

NOTES

NOTES

Writing leaflets
for patients

Guidelines for producing written information

Jenny Secker and Rachel Pollard

Health Education Board
for Scotland

ISBN:1 873 452 71 3

Typeset in Times New Roman 12 on 14pt

Designed by Mark Blackadder

Health Education Board for Scotland
Woodburn House
Canaan Lane
Edinburgh
EH10 4SG